FROM BUGBOTS TO HUMANOIDS

ROBOTICS

Library of Congress Cataloging-in-Publication Data

Strom, Laura Layton.
   From bugbots to humanoids : robotics / By Laura Layton Strom.
      p. cm. -- (Shockwave)
   Includes index.
   ISBN-10: 0-531-17585-5 (lib. bdg.)
   ISBN-13: 978-0-531-17585-9 (lib. bdg.)
   ISBN-10: 0-531-18843-4 (pbk.)
   ISBN-13: 978-0-531-18843-9 (pbk.)
 1. Robotics--Juvenile literature. 2. Robots--Design and
construction--Juvenile literature. I. Title.

 TJ211.2.S77 2007
 629.8'92--dc22

2007019985

Published in 2008 by Children's Press, an imprint of Scholastic Inc.,
557 Broadway, New York, New York 10012
www.scholastic.com

SCHOLASTIC, CHILDREN'S PRESS, and associated logos are trademarks
and/or registered trademarks of Scholastic Inc.

08 09 10 11 12 13 14 15 16 17
10 9 8 7 6 5 4 3 2 1

Printed in China through Colorcraft Ltd., Hong Kong

Author: Laura Layton Strom
Educational Consultant: Ian Morrison
Editor: Frances Chan
Designer: Matthew Alexander
Photo Researchers: Jamshed Mistry and Frances Chan

Photographs by: Big Stock Photo (pp. 3–5; p. 34); **Courtesy of Ben Sweeney and dedicated
to Dolores Sweeney/www.leonardoshands.com** (robot knight, p. 11); **Courtesy of C. J. Chung,
Lawrence Tech University/www.robofest.net** (RoboFest competition, p. 29); **Courtesy of
Dr. David Hanson/www.hansonrobotics.com** (K-bot, p. 27); **Courtesy of Dr. Gavin Miller 2006/
www.snakerobots.com** (snake robot, p. 19); **Donna Coveney/MIT** (Cynthia Breazeal and Kismet,
p. 31); **Getty Images** (p. 16; woman driving, p. 29; p. 30; human and robotic hands, pp. 32–33);
Greenhill Photo Library (shadow hand robot, p. 17); **NASA/Johnson Space Center** (spiderbot,
Hubble, p. 21); **Photolibrary** (pp. 7–9; car-assembly plant, robots welding, pp. 12–13; NASA
Robonaut, p. 20; Cassini, p. 21; p. 22; nanorobot, p. 29); **Rex Features** (Robug, p. 13); **Stockbyte/
John Foxx Images** (cover); **Tranz/Corbis** (p. 10; Mobot, p. 11; p. 14; robotic arms, long-distance
surgery, p. 17; pp. 22–23; p. 25; Asimo robot, p. 27; Dr. Cynthia Breazeal, p. 31); **Tranz/Reuters**
(robot waiters, p. 13; p. 15; pp. 18–19; pp. 24–25; Repliee Q2, p. 31); **United States Airforce**
(p. 28)

All illustrations and other photographs © Weldon Owen Education Inc.

SHOCKWAVE
SCIENCE

FROM BUGBOTS TO HUMANOIDS

ROBOTICS

Laura Layton Strom

children's press®

An imprint of Scholastic Inc.

NEW YORK • TORONTO • LONDON • AUCKLAND • SYDNEY
MEXICO CITY • NEW DELHI • HONG KONG
DANBURY, CONNECTICUT

CHECK THESE OUT!

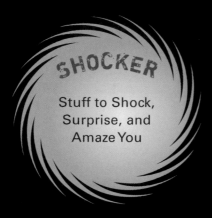

SHOCKER

Stuff to Shock,
Surprise, and
Amaze You

Quick Recaps
and Notable
Notes

Word Stunners
and Other Oddities

The Heads-Up
on Expert Reading

Links to More
Information

CONTENTS

animatronics (*AN uh muh TRON iks*) creating motion in puppets with robotic technology or a robotic technology used to control the motions of puppets

artificial intelligence the capability of a computer or robot to learn from its environment; the science of inventing beings with this capability

automaton (*aw TOM uh ton*) self-operating machines, especially those that are not powered by electronics

bugbot a robot that is designed to move like an insect

cyborg (*SYE borg*) a human being with robotic or electronic implants

humanoid a being with human-like body features, such as an android or a gorilla

· ·

For additional vocabulary, see Glossary on page 34.

> The *-oid* suffix on words such as *android* and *humanoid* means "like" or "resembling." Similar words include: *spheroid, anthropoid,* and *trapezoid.*

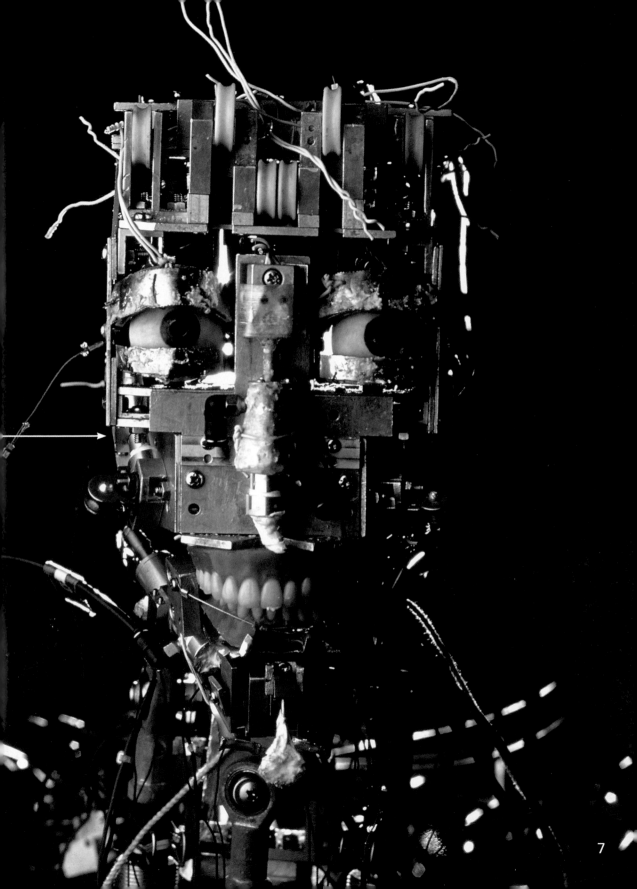

Humans have been building robots for over 2,000 years. Early robots, called **automatons**, were powered by wind-up gears. Modern robots are electronically powered. Some robots have **sensors**. They are programmed to avoid obstacles or perform tasks. Security robots are programmed to sense changes in the atmosphere. They will act if they sense hazards, such as fire, smoke, chemicals, or flooding.

The field of robotics is changing rapidly. New ideas are proposed every day. Some scientists are trying to build robots with **artificial intelligence**. These robots would be able to adapt to new situations, and learn on their own. Maybe they will be able to have real conversations with humans. In fact, scientists can't even agree on how to define artificial intelligence!

There is no one view on what a robot is, either. If a machine can move on its own, some people call it a robot. Others say a robot needs to be able perform tasks, and use **logic**. Some people say just use common sense to determine whether a machine can be called a robot. What do you think?

Some Robot Firsts ▼

1921
Czech writer Karel Capek introduces the word *robot* in his play *R.U.R.* (*Rossum's Universal Robots*).

1962
General Motors uses the first industrial arm robot in car manufacturing – the Unimate.

1977
Robot explorers *Voyager 1* and *Voyager 2* are launched into space to probe the solar system.

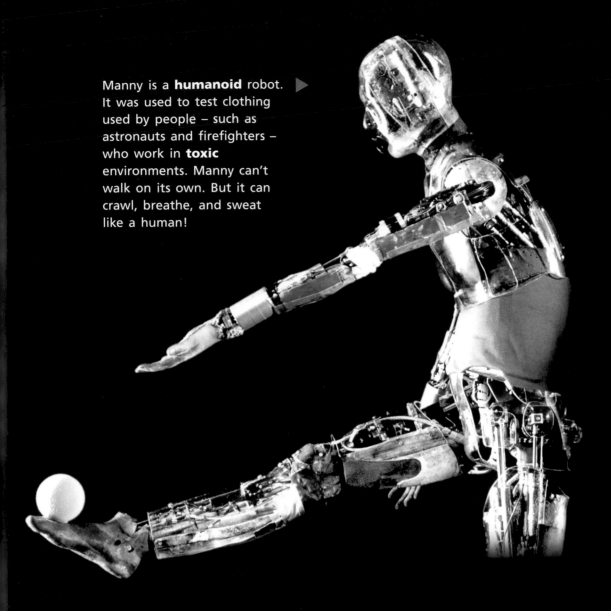

Manny is a **humanoid** robot. It was used to test clothing used by people – such as astronauts and firefighters – who work in **toxic** environments. Manny can't walk on its own. But it can crawl, breathe, and sweat like a human!

1993

Dante, an eight-legged robot, is sent to collect data in the crater of Mount Erebus in Antarctica.

1994

VaMP and VITA-2, the first robot cars, take a drive in Paris, reaching speeds of up to 80 miles per hour.

2005

Honda introduces new Asimo, the latest version of its humanoid robot.

From Dreams to Automatons

Since ancient times, human imagination has crafted dreams of robotic assistants that can do any number of tasks. In 322 B.C., Greek philosopher Aristotle (*AR is staht uhl*) wrote that if tools could do work when ordered, there would be no need for **apprentices** or slaves. The Greeks created the first automatons in the first century B.C. They designed water clocks with automatic moving parts. During the eighteenth and nineteenth centuries, automaton makers designed wind-up toys and mechanical clocks. But these **civilizations** did not have the **technology** that we have now. The automatons did not have intelligence or sensing capability. Nor could they do more than one task.

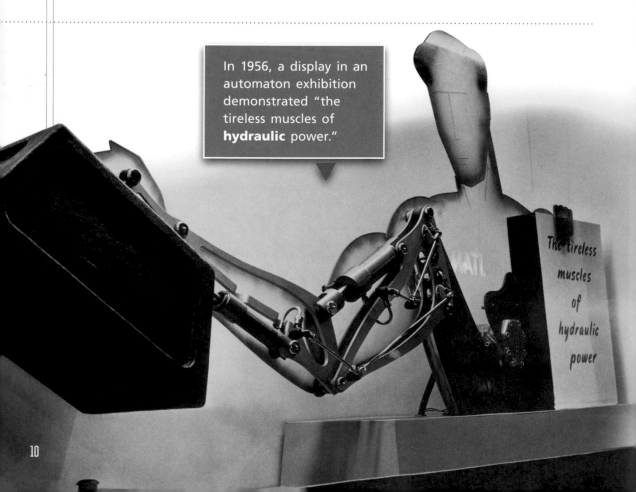

In 1956, a display in an automaton exhibition demonstrated "the tireless muscles of **hydraulic** power."

The tireless muscles of hydraulic power

Industrial robots were introduced in the 1950s. These robots could lift heavy loads repeatedly without tiring like a human. In the 1960s, robots got sensors and cameras. In the 1980s, the high cost of human labor in Europe led to further development of human-like robots to replace factory workers. Robots became able to respond to voices and words. As computer technology developed, so did the abilities of robots.

In 1965, the Hughes Aircraft Company started using Mobot in areas too hazardous for humans to work in. Mobot could crawl along the ocean floor and handle radioactive materials in laboratories.

The First Robot?

In 1495, Italian artist and inventor Leonardo da Vinci sketched designs for a knight. The knight moved with disks, gears, and pulleys. Though da Vinci never built his design, a group of engineers did so in 2003. Incredibly, the knight could sit, stand, and move its neck, arms, and jaw. So da Vinci designed an early version of a robot more than five hundred years ago!

Leonardo's knight

Job Opening: Robot

Could we live without robots today? Robots do many jobs that people would prefer not to do. For example, robots do repetitive tasks, such as screwing on bottle caps, cutting parts, or stacking products round the clock. Robots on assembly lines do everything from package peanut butter to build robots. Other robots explore shipwrecks and study sea life on the ocean floor. They can work in pressures that would crush a human body.

Fans of robots say that robots make manufacturing cleaner and safer. Humans spread germs, and shed dead skin, hair, and clothing fibers. Robots do none of these things. And they never make mistakes. Robots don't need vacations or lunch breaks either!

> The opening sentence is asking a question. I don't think the author really expects an answer. It is just her way of getting the reader to think about the topic.

Robots are used in many stages of car manufacturing, from transporting heavy parts along the assembly line (left) to welding the frame together (right).

Robots in airports can clean floors 24 hours a day.

▲ Creepy Crawlies

Many robot scientists, or roboticists, study the movement of insects and other small creatures when designing their robots. That's why the machines they create are often called **bugbots**. Engineers at the University of Portsmouth in England looked at crabs and spiders for inspiration when designing Robug III (above). Robug can step over large obstacles. It can climb up walls using its vacuum gripper feet, which work even on rough surfaces, such as brick. It can move as quickly as 20 feet per minute. Robug is connected to a human operator by a 328-foot cable. The cable includes a compressed-air hose, which powers the legs.

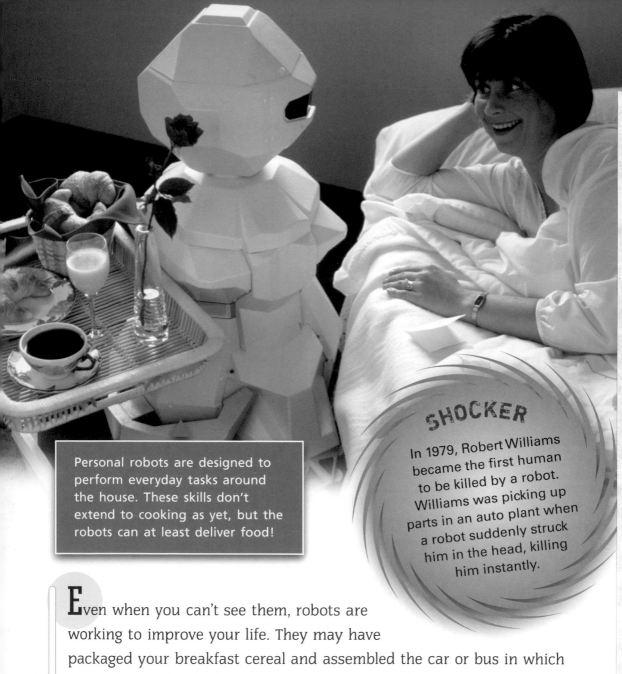

Personal robots are designed to perform everyday tasks around the house. These skills don't extend to cooking as yet, but the robots can at least deliver food!

SHOCKER

In 1979, Robert Williams became the first human to be killed by a robot. Williams was picking up parts in an auto plant when a robot suddenly struck him in the head, killing him instantly.

Even when you can't see them, robots are working to improve your life. They may have packaged your breakfast cereal and assembled the car or bus in which you rode to school. There may be robotic technology in your car, improving its steering and operating its **navigation** system.

Some people own personal robots that vacuum floors, mow lawns, and guard against fire and intruders. When sensing danger, a guard robot can send a warning message to the owner's cell phone. Some guard robots have cameras so that the owner can see what the robot is seeing.

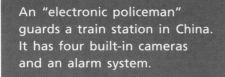

An "electronic policeman" guards a train station in China. It has four built-in cameras and an alarm system.

报警按钮 ●ALARM

话筒　MIC

武汉市公安局监制

警用设施

Robots – Advantages

- will do repetitive jobs
- work in hazardous conditions
- don't need time off
- never get sick
- don't spread germs

May I Take ◄ Your Order?

At Robot Kitchen in Hong Kong, China, robots work as waiters. Robo Waiter 1 takes orders, and sends them to the kitchen by infrared signals. Robo Waiter 2 delivers the meals to the right tables. The robots' built-in cameras ensure that they don't collide with customers or furniture. They can work nonstop for 10 hours between battery charges. The restaurant owner has ordered a third robot to work in the kitchen. It will be programmed to flip burgers and cook omelets.

Limbs and Laboratories

Increasingly, people who lose limbs are able to walk and reach again, thanks to robotics. In fact, scientists hope that someday nobody will ever have to use a wheelchair! Robotic body parts may someday be the solution for people injured in accidents or those born with physical challenges.

"Hello, I'm Dr. Robot!" Maybe you'll hear that soon! Amazingly, robots are already in hospitals doing delicate surgery with the help of a human surgeon. Robotic tools smaller than a human finger can cut and mend skin or internal organs. A camera on the tool lets the surgeon watch the procedure on a computer screen. The surgeon can use a joystick to guide the robot.

Robots are also used in science laboratories to measure liquids. Since a robot cannot get sick, robots often handle germs or dangerous chemicals, and work in **radioactive** areas.

American Bill Dunham is the first amputee to be fitted with a motorized artificial leg. It reacts to his movements to create a more natural stride and restore muscle power.

▲ Pump It Up

The Shadow Hand can pick up an egg without breaking it! Developed by the Shadow Robot Company in England, the hand has the same joints as a human hand. It can be used in many applications, such as handling fragile or dangerous objects. The Shadow Hand can be used with the Shadow Air Muscle. This robotic forearm consists of rubber tubes covered in tough plastic netting. Move a lever and the "muscles" inflate with compressed air, which causes them to contract.

The first laboratory robots had arms like these to work with dangerous materials. The scientist moves the arms using a remote control behind protective glass.

Long-distance surgery has been performed with the help of a remote-controlled robot. This doctor is in New York, but he is doing surgery on his patient in France!

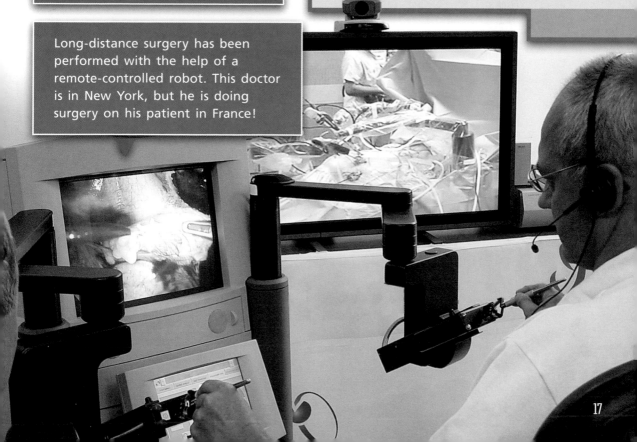

DEPTHX is an underwater robot. NASA is testing it in one of the world's deepest sinkholes in Mexico. In the future, NASA aims to send it to search for life on Europa, Jupiter's icy moon.

Boiling, Freezing, Toxic, Stinky!

If a job is boiling, freezing, toxic, or stinky, some say send in a robot! Robots survey volcanoes, earthquake faults, and stinky sewers. Robots are sent on long voyages through the solar system to photograph distant planets. These robots are built to withstand the harsh radiation and extreme temperatures of outer space. Solar power or **plutonium** batteries can keep them running for decades.

Robots were used to help clean up the nuclear reactor disaster in Chernobyl in the former Soviet Union. They were also used to search for survivors in the World Trade Center rubble after the terrorist attack on September 11, 2001. Robots also work to search for and **defuse** bombs.

DEPTHX and NASA are both acronyms – words created by using the beginning letters of other words. Other common acronyms include: RAM, NATO, and SCUBA.

Guardrobo D1 patrols a building in Tokyo looking for water leakage or fire. If it detects fire, it will extinguish it.

Smart Snakes ▶

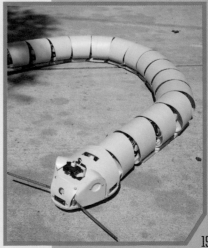

Dr. Gavin Miller has developed a series of snake robots. Why snakes? Dr. Miller has observed that snakes are well designed to survive in many environments. Their elongated spines allow them to hunt in tunnels, above the ground, in dry or wet terrain, and even in trees. Dr. Miller is hoping that his devices can be used in search-and-rescue missions. Imagine snakebots slithering into tight areas looking for survivors in the aftermath of an earthquake. The robots could also take supplies to trapped people. This **prototype** has a video camera and many sensors in its head. A finished version will have a covering to protect the parts from dirt.

Neither Air Nor Gravity!

Outer space is a difficult place for humans, who need oxygen and moderate temperatures. But robots don't need oxygen. They can withstand solar flares and freezing temperatures, and don't mind long trips.

In 1966, before humans went to the moon, a robot probe named *Surveyor* explored the moon's surface. It took thousands of pictures that provided information for the astronauts who first walked on the moon in 1969. In 1997, *Sojourner* became the first robot to go to another planet. This shoebox-sized rover robot had wheels. It bumped along the surface of Mars taking pictures. Its robotic arm scooped up samples of rocks and soil.

The *Cassini* spacecraft was launched in 1997. It entered Saturn's orbit in 2004. The spacecraft has several robotic sensing instruments on board. It can "see" light at wavelengths that the human eye can't detect. *Cassini* also dropped a robotic laboratory on the surface of Titan, Saturn's largest moon.

NASA's Robonaut is controlled remotely by a human operator. The operator wears a motion-sensitive glove and a headset, which sees through Robonaut's two camera eyes. Robonaut is designed to do tasks inside and outside the International Space Station.

Lending an Arm ▶

Probably the most-used robot in space is the Remote Manipulator System (RMS). Also known as the Canadarm, it has been on more than 50 space-shuttle missions since 1981. The RMS arm is 50 feet long, and is capable of lifting 65,000 pounds in space. It has six joints similar to the joints in a human arm. In 2001, Canadarm2 was launched. It is a more advanced robotic arm that is used on the International Space Station.

An astronaut on the end of the RMS is carried to the top of the Hubble Space Telescope to do some maintenance work.

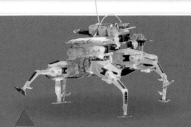

NASA's prototype spiderbot can fit in the palm of an adult's hand. Spiderbots are intended to be used to explore and collect data on other planets. In the future, a hundred or more spiderbots may be programmed to work together on tasks such as digging or repairing.

The heading, combined with what I have already read, makes me think that these pages will be about the use of robots in space. It sure helps to be able to predict what will be on the page.

This artist's impression shows *Cassini* orbiting Saturn. The spacecraft had to slip between Saturn's rings in order to enter orbit.

Robo-Characters

Maid? Companion? Superhero? Villain? Robot characters are part of popular culture. Most have special strengths, such as the ability to run faster or hear or see better. Whether friendly and helpful or **menacing** and destructive, robots have been entertaining us and frightening us in books and movies since the 1920s.

Probably the most well-known robot characters in movie history are R2-D2 and **android** C-3PO from the Star Wars series.

The Jurassic Park ride at Universal Studios, California, features a robotic Tyrannosaurus rex.

Some fantasy characters that you see in movies, museums, and amusement parks are controlled by robotics. **Animatronics** is the name for advanced puppetry combined with robotics. The term comes from the word *audio-animatronics*, first used in the 1960s to describe the moving models on display at Disneyland. In filmmaking during this time, mechanical models used basic robot technology. As the making of special effects has grown into a billion-dollar industry, animatronics have become much more **sophisticated**. Animatronic robots usually cannot move on their own. Their motions are controlled by human puppeteers, but they look and act like living creatures.

Hi-tech animatronics were used for the close-ups of King Kong and the dinosaur in the 2005 movie *King Kong*.

Robot Rules

Isaac Asimov was a science fiction and popular science writer. He wrote or edited more than 500 fiction and nonfiction books. His 1950 series, *I, Robot* featured The Three Laws of Robotics. This list greatly influenced other science-fiction writers.

The Three Laws of Robotics:

1 A robot may not injure a human being, or through inaction allow a human being to come to harm.

2 A robot must obey the orders given to it by human beings, except where such orders would conflict with the First Law.

3 A robot must protect its own existence as long as such protection does not conflict with the First or Second Law.

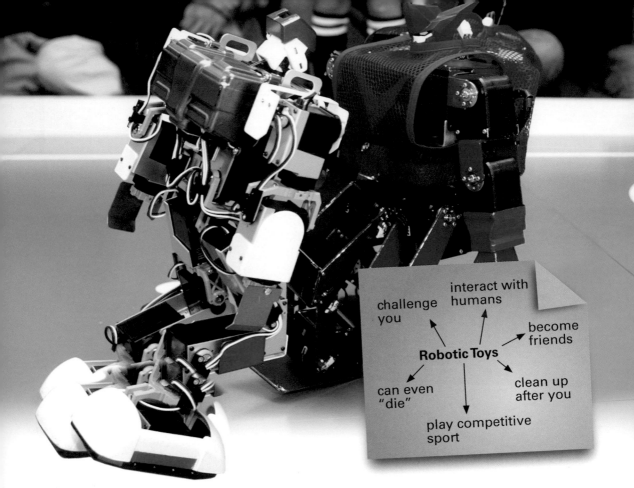

challenge
you

interact with
humans

become
friends

Robotic Toys

can even
"die"

clean up
after you

play competitive
sport

Robot Playmates

Have you ever wanted a robot companion? Who wouldn't want a robot friend that would also make the bed and take out the garbage? Wouldn't it be great to have a robot pet that you did not have to clean up after?

Some new robotic toys are designed to interact with humans. The toy may recognize voices and respond with words, singing, smiling, and even dancing. Some robot toys will "die" if they are ignored. Designers think that these robots can help teach children responsibility.

Other robots play competitive sports. Roboticists have created small robots that can kick soccer balls and aim for goals. Fans of robo-soccer gather for the RoboCup tournament, held in different parts of the world each year.

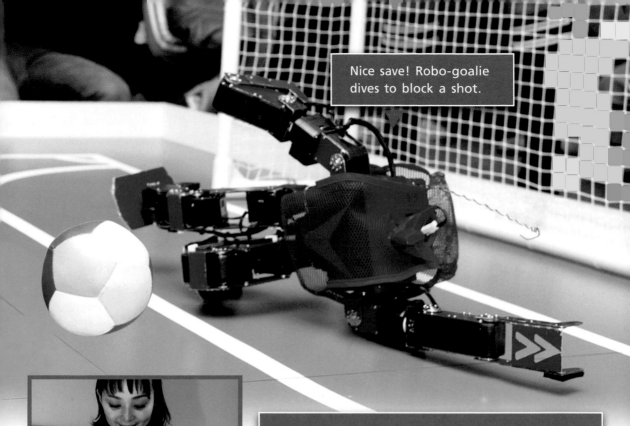

Nice save! Robo-goalie dives to block a shot.

In many ways, a NeCoRo acts like a real cat. It recognizes its own name when called. It purrs when it is petted or held. It will get angry if someone is violent toward it. NeCoRo also decides when it wants to sleep or to cuddle.

Super Computers ▶

Some machines can play chess and other strategy games. In 1997, world champion Gary Kasparov faced IBM's Deep Blue in one of the most famous chess matches ever. Because Deep Blue cannot move, it isn't a robot, but a highly advanced computer program. It could evaluate 200 million positions per second. Deep Blue's victory marked the first time a computer had ever defeated a grand master of chess. Kasparov accused Deep Blue of cheating and demanded a rematch. But IBM retired the program. Today, computer programs consistently defeat grand masters. They can even invent strategies that surprise their programmers!

An audience watches a live broadcast of the chess game between Kasparov and Deep Blue.

Cyborgs and Humanoids

Fictional **cyborgs** are often killing machines disguised to look like humans. But real-life cyborgs exist. They are ordinary people who are aided by special electrical devices in their bodies, such as cochlear (*KOKE lee er*) implants. A cochlear implant is an electronic device placed in the skull of a person who is deaf or almost deaf. Unlike a hearing aid, which makes sounds louder, the implant bypasses the damaged parts of the ear and stimulates a functioning nerve in the ear so that the person can hear sounds and speech. Similar cyborg technology is also being tested on people who are paralyzed. An electronic device **mimics** brain signals to produce movement in a person's muscles. With **rehabilitation**, the person can learn to stand and walk.

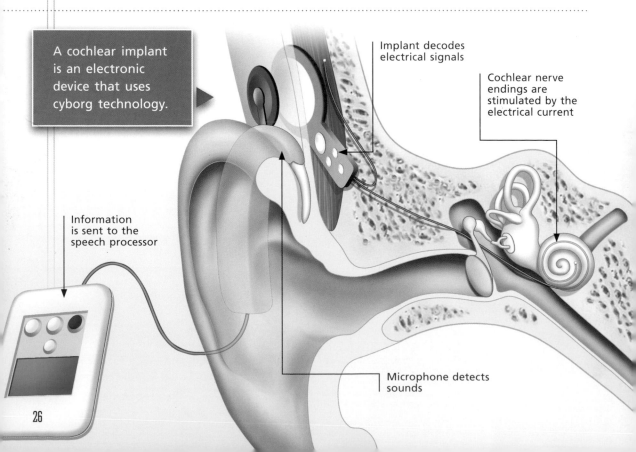

A cochlear implant is an electronic device that uses cyborg technology.

Implant decodes electrical signals

Cochlear nerve endings are stimulated by the electrical current

Information is sent to the speech processor

Microphone detects sounds

Humanoids, or robosapiens, are robots that look and act like a human. A perfect robot person does not yet exist. However, scientists are creating robots that can recognize faces and voices, walk, dance, climb stairs, sing, play games, and imitate a person's actions. Someday scientists want to create a humanoid who can think on its own.

Sapiens in the word *robosapiens* is from the Latin "to be wise" or "to think." Our own species *homosapiens* means "thinking man." New toys include: *Spidersapiens* (spiderman) and even *Homersapiens* (from *The Simpsons*).

▲ Facing the Future

Roboticist Dr. David Hanson created this advanced face robot called K-bot. Behind its foam-rubber skin is a network of wires, 24 tiny motors, and two cameras. K-bot has 28 realistic facial expressions. It is programmed to learn in a natural way, and to recognize and respond to people. Its eyes can follow a person around a room, and it can imitate what it sees. The next step for Hanson is to add a speaker that can create speech.

Japanese schoolchildren copy Asimo, the humanoid, as it balances on one leg. Asimo is used to help teach science topics, such as gravity and robotic technology.

Robots of the Future

Every year, Americans waste millions of hours and gallons of fuel waiting in traffic jams. Researchers are working on robotic cars coupled with an automated highway system. This could prevent traffic congestion and crashes. A network of computers in the roadway and in the robotic cars would control speed and the interval between cars. Everyone would travel smoothly and take up less space. Sensors in each robotic car would help keep the car in its lane. Robotics would aid steering, braking, and navigating toward the car's destination.

We may see pilotless passenger planes in the future. Unmanned planes already exist in the military. They are used to survey dangerous areas, spy, and check weather patterns. Some can even fire missiles.

The *Predator* is a remotely piloted aircraft. One pilot and two sensor operators fly the robot from a ground control station. The U.S. military uses *Predator* to find and attack enemy troops.

The i-unit is a personal vehicle that enables the passenger to move quickly through crowds. When the vehicle reclines, it can move at higher speeds. The i-unit can sense and avoid people and other obstacles. It can be steered or put on autopilot for an accident-free journey.

◀ Future Talent

RoboFest is an international competition for robot lovers in grades 5 to 12. At RoboFest, kids have the chance to show off robots they have designed, constructed, and programmed. At a past RoboFest, one robot made hamburgers and another played the piano! RoboFest offers a fun environment where students learn problem-solving techniques, mathematics, creativity, physics, electronics, teamwork, and computer programming.

339-3

The race is on to create the **molecular** technology necessary to build **nanorobots.** These robots are microscopic machines that could offer numerous medical and industrial applications. They are also called nanobots, nanoids, and nanites.

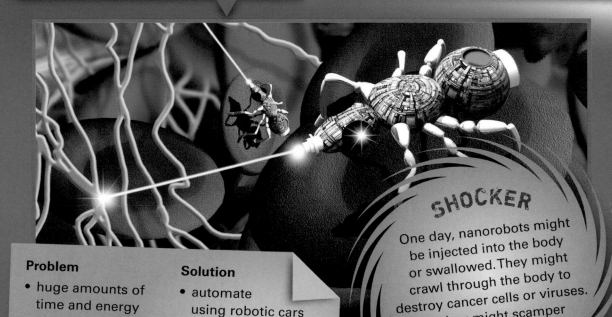

Problem
- huge amounts of time and energy wasted in traffic jams
- some flights can be very dangerous

Solution
- automate using robotic cars and systems
- use newly developed unmanned planes

SHOCKER
One day, nanorobots might be injected into the body or swallowed. They might crawl through the body to destroy cancer cells or viruses. Or they might scamper through the arteries to break up clots!

Most helper robots today do one task, but scientists are working on robots that can do multiple tasks. For example, we may soon have a robot that unloads the dishwasher and puts the dishes away. In the near future, scientists predict we will be able to purchase a robot that will clean the house and wash the car!

Artificial intelligence (AI) is the science of creating machines that can replicate human thought and decision making. AI may someday make robots think like humans and have conversations like humans. Some scientists predict that a robot as smart as a human will be built before the year 2050. To get to that stage, scientists are designing robots that learn by making mistakes, and may some day be able to consider consequences before making a mistake. To be considered human-like, a robot would also need to have goals, beliefs, feelings, and preferences.

Robot Action Painter (RAP) is an artist! It chooses its own colors and paints until it decides the picture is complete. Then it will put its unique RAP signature on the bottom.

SHOCKER

For robots to live independently of humans, they need a way to renew their own energy. One way scientists have found to solve this is by having a robot eat flies! In order to attract flies, the scientists smear excrement on the robot!

If you could look into the future, would you picture robots cleaning your house, changing your children's diapers, or baking your favorite dessert? Or would you see robots as something to be feared? Could superhuman robots be more dangerous than helpful?

Kismet

▼ Leading the Way

Dr. Cynthia Breazeal (below) is a roboticist and AI expert. She has developed several projects, including Cog, an upper-torso humanoid, and Kismet, a highly expressive robotic face. Her research programs aim to create cooperative and capable robots that can work and learn in partnership with people. She is pictured with a robotic flower, which bends when touched by human hands.

Who is real and who is a robot? Repliee Q2 is a highly advanced android. Her body has 42 sensors and motors to generate human-like behavior. She can flutter her eyelids and even appear to breathe. Her flexible silicone skin is soft to touch. Repliee is on the left.

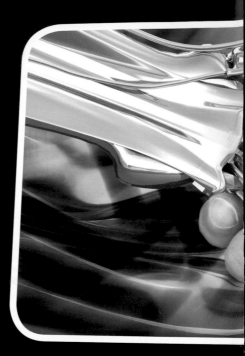

Artificial intelligence may someday make robots think and communicate like humans. In contrast, scientists are also developing cyborg technology to enhance humans with robotic parts. A "posthuman" could be made up of human and artificial intelligence. Nanobots working inside a body could keep a person youthful and healthy indefinitely.

WHAT DO YOU THINK?

Do you think it's a good idea to make robots that can think for themselves and survive on their own?

PRO

I think we should continue to experiment with using robots to help us improve our society. Anything that helps us understand ourselves and build a safer world is all right by me. It is natural for humans to want to advance their knowledge and technology.

AFTERSHOCKS

Some scientists believe these advanced robotic parts are a realistic replacement for devices we use now, such as contact lenses and hearing aids. They could also replace cosmetic surgery procedures. In the future, a person could possibly order robotic eyes or even a new heart!

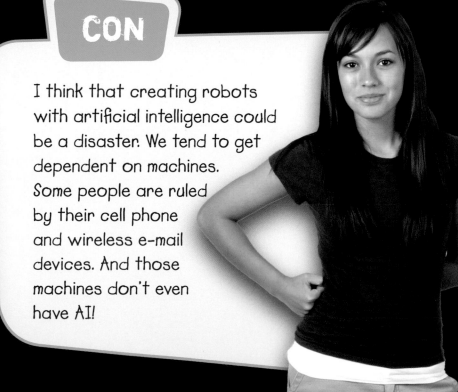

CON

I think that creating robots with artificial intelligence could be a disaster. We tend to get dependent on machines. Some people are ruled by their cell phone and wireless e-mail devices. And those machines don't even have AI!

GLOSSARY

android a robot designed to look and behave like a human

apprentice a person who learns a trade by working with a skilled person in that trade

civilization a highly developed and organized society

defuse (*dee FYOOZ*) to alter a bomb so it cannot explode

hydraulic (*hye DRAW lik*) operated on power created when liquid is forced under pressure through pipes

logic (*LOJ ik*) thinking that involves reasoning and following steps

menacing (*MEN iss ing*) threatening

mimic to imitate something else's motion or speech patterns

molecular (*muh LEK yuh ler*) relating to molecules, the smallest particle into which a substance can be divided while still being the same substance

nanorobot an extremely small robot that can be seen only under a microscope

navigation (*nav uh GAY shun*) finding the way when traveling, often with the help of maps, compasses, or the stars

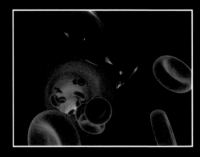

Nanorobots

plutonium a radioactive element that releases energy as it decays

prototype (*PROH tuh tipe*) the first version of an invention, which tests whether it will work

radioactive (*ray dee oh AK tiv*) giving off harmful radiation

rehabilitation (*ree huh bil i TAY shun*) a process of restoring a person to good health

sensor (*SEN sur*) an instrument that responds to or detects heat, sound, or pressure

sophisticated (*suh FISS tuh kay tid*) cleverly designed and able to do complicated things

technology the application of knowledge within a specific field, such as robotics

toxic (*TOK sik*) poisonous

FIND OUT MORE

BOOKS

Bridgman, Roger Francis. *Robot*. DK Eyewitness Books, 2004.

Domaine, Helena. *Robotics*. Lerner Publishing Company, 2005.

Gifford, Clive. *How the Future Began: Machines*. Kingfisher, 2000.

Margulies, Phillip. *Artificial Intelligence*. Blackbirch Press, 2003.

Somervill, Barbara A. *The History of the Computer*. Child's World, 2006.

Tambini, Michael. *Future*. DK Eyewitness Books, 2002.

WEB SITES

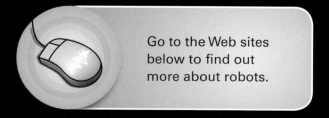

Go to the Web sites below to find out more about robots.

www.thetech.org/robotics

www.robofest.net

www.pbs.org/wgbh/nova/robots/hazard

http://library.thinkquest.org/2705

INDEX

ABOUT THE AUTHOR

Laura Layton Strom is the author of many fiction and nonfiction books for children. She has worked as an educational writer, editor, and publisher for more than 20 years. Laura has always been fascinated by robots on TV and in movies. She hopes to have her very own robot one day that will clean the house and pick up after the dog!